GREEN BOND MARKET SURVEY FOR THE PHILIPPINES

INSIGHTS ON THE PERSPECTIVES OF INSTITUTIONAL INVESTORS AND UNDERWRITERS

JULY 2022

ASIAN DEVELOPMENT BANK

ADB

CONTENTS

TABLE, FIGURES, AND BOXES

BOXES

ACKNOWLEDGMENTS

The lead authors—Kosintr Puongsophol, financial sector specialist; Oth Marulou Gagni, senior operations assistant; and Alita Lestor, consultant; all from the Economic Research and Regional Cooperation Department (ERCD) of the Asian Development Bank—would like to particularly thank Satoru Yamadera, advisor, ERCD; Richard Supangan, senior economics officer, ERCD; Noel Peters, principal investment specialist (climate finance), Private Sector Operations Department (PSOD); Daniel Wiedmer, principal investment specialist, PSOD; Alix Burrell, principal investment specialist, PSOD; and Rafael Montinola, Investment specialist, PSOD for their support and contributions. Editing was done by Kevin Donahue. Design and layout by Prince Nicdao.

The lead authors would like to thank the Global Green Growth Institute team—comprising Srinath Komarina, Hien Tran, Thinh Tran, Minh Tran, and Ha Nguyen—for their inputs and suggestions.

Finally, we would like to express our heartfelt gratitude to the Philippine regulatory authorities and industry associations, as well as to all respondents, for their assistance with and participation in the survey. The local regulatory authorities include the Bangko Sentral ng Pilipinas, Insurance Commission, and Securities and Exchange Commission. Industry associations include the Bankers Association of the Philippines, Philippine Insurers and Reinsurers Association, and Philippine Life Insurance Association, Inc.

ABBREVIATIONS

ABMI	ASEAN+3 Asian Bond Markets Initiative
ADB	Asian Development Bank
ASEAN	Association of Southeast Asian Nations
ASEAN+3	ASEAN plus the People's Republic of China, Japan, and the Republic of Korea
BIS	Bank for International Settlements
BSP	Bangko Sentral ng Pilipinas
ESG	environmental, social, and governance
LCY	local currency
NGFS	Network of Central Banks and Supervisors for Greening the Financial System
PLC	publicly listed company
SEC	Securities and Exchange Commission
USD	United States dollar

SUMMARY AND KEY FINDINGS

SURVEY HIGHLIGHTS

In January 2022, the Asian Development Bank and the Global Green Growth Institute conducted an online survey and received a total of 48 responses from institutional investors and underwriters in the Philippines. The survey was conducted to assess institutional investors' interest in green bonds issued in the Philippines, as well as the perspectives of local underwriters on their clients' interest in green bond issuance. The survey identified the market drivers, impediments, and development priorities for the Philippines' sustainable finance market to assist development partners in identifying potential areas of support to accelerate the development of the Philippines' sustainable finance market. The most noteworthy survey findings are presented below:

► While all respondents (investors and underwriters) expressed interest in investing in and underwriting green bonds, the majority have limited awareness and resources. This is an area where development partners such as the Asian Development Bank can support interested entities with technical assistance and capacity building.

► Renewable energy, green buildings, sustainable agriculture, and water management are viewed as the most promising sectors for growth in the Philippines' green bond market.

► While there is a strong preference for small green projects (less than USD10 million) from investors' point of view, underwriters and advisors, on average, are seeking much bigger deals (more than USD100 million).

► Both investors and underwriters consider the lack of understanding of the clear benefits of green bonds, compared with conventional bonds, as a major impediment to the green bond market's development in the Philippines.

► While nearly 51% of investors believe that embedding the Sustainable Development Goals in investment strategies is critical for investing in green bonds, 67% of underwriters believe that attracting new investors is the key motivation for green bond issuance.

► Development banks can play a variety of roles in catalyzing growth in the green bond market.

The green bond market in the Philippines has potential to expand further. The majority of institutional investors and underwriters are interested in green bonds. However, they have limited awareness and resources to expand their green portfolios and underwrite more green bonds.

Renewable energy, green buildings, sustainable agriculture, and water management are the sectors with the highest growth potential. Survey respondents agreed on the importance and potential of renewable energy, green buildings, sustainable agriculture, and water management. Indeed, some of these sectors already account for the majority of investors' portfolios in the Philippine green bond market (**Table**). Meanwhile, 23% of the institutional investors surveyed had no exposure to green bonds.

Table: The Philippines' Green Bond Market—Share of Investor and Underwriter Portfolio Exposure by Sector
(%)

Investors			Underwriters		
Renewable Energy	No Exposure to Green Bonds	Water Management	Renewable Energy	Green Buildings	Sustainable Agriculture
32	23	13	23	23	15

Source: Authors' compilation based on survey results.

A clear investment mandate and the expansion of eligible issuers are needed to increase investment. More than 51% of survey respondents believed that to increase investment in green bonds, investors must incorporate environmental, social, and governance principles and the Sustainable Development Goals into their investment strategies. Meanwhile, both underwriters and investors shared the view that it is critical to put in place tax incentives or subsidies for green bond issuers and investors to deepen the Philippine green bond market. Governments and regulators can catalyze the market's development by incentivizing investors and improving disclosure requirements.

Increased demand from investors is extremely important. Underwriters believed that increased demand from investors is crucial to encourage more issuance of green bonds. In fact, preferential buying by public pension funds and central banks would demonstrate leading by example. They also believe that tax incentives and/or subsidies for issuers are equally important.

Unlike underwriters, investors have a strong preference for smaller investment sizes. Almost 67% of investors are seeking to invest less than USD10 million per green bond transaction, while only 13% are interested in investing up to USD50 million. On the other hand, almost 67% of underwriters are looking for green bond issuance sizes of more than USD100 million.

Investing in and issuing green bonds improves an organization's image. Nearly all investors and underwriters agreed that investing in and issuing green bonds can help an organization improve its green image. From an investor's point of view, investing in green bonds allows them to better diversify their portfolios, while issuers hope that issuing green bonds will result in lower funding costs, albeit not immediately but potentially in the long run.

External review is needed to create more demand. Nearly 58% of investors believe that an external review report is necessary for making informed investment decisions. Based on survey responses, the increased use of external review would help issuers to diversify their investor base.

Development partners can play an important role in promoting green finance. All respondents agreed that development partners such as the Asian Development Bank (ADB) can play a variety of roles in assisting the Philippine green finance market's development. Along with serving as a knowledge partner, ADB can provide technical assistance to assist local companies in issuing green bonds and identifying eligible green projects and expenditures. Additionally, ADB can invest in green bonds and/or make green loans to domestic entities.

INTRODUCTION

Background and Objective

The Asian Development Bank (ADB) is collaborating closely with the Association of Southeast Asian Nations (ASEAN), the People's Republic of China, Japan, and the Republic of Korea—collectively known as ASEAN+3—to promote the development of local currency (LCY) bond markets and regional bond market integration through the Asian Bond Markets Initiative (ABMI). ABMI was established in 2002 to bolster the resilience of ASEAN+3 financial systems by developing LCY bond markets as an alternative source to foreign currency-denominated, short-term bank loans for long-term investment financing.

ADB, as Secretariat for the ABMI, is implementing a regional technical assistance program to promote sustainable LCY bond market development with support from the People's Republic of China Povery Reduction and Regional Cooperation Fund. This technical assistance was developed and is being implemented with guidance from ASEAN+3 finance ministers and central bank governors, and in accordance with the ABMI Medium-Term Road Map for 2019–2022.

This survey report, conducted in collaboration with the Global Green Growth Institute, aims to assess institutional investors' interest in green bonds issued in the Philippines, as well as the perspectives of local arrangers and underwriters on their clients' interest in green bond issuance. The survey aims to identify market drivers, impediments, and development priorities for the Philippines' sustainable finance market to assist development partners in identifying potential areas of support to accelerate the development of the Philippines' sustainable finance market.

Methodologies

In January 2022, ADB and the Global Green Growth Institute conducted the survey via an online platform and received a total of 48 responses from 1 asset management firm, 10 brokerage firms (proprietary trading), 1 commercial and corporate lending bank, 18 commercial banks (treasury) including thrift and universal banks, 1 trust department, 3 financial advisors and underwriters, 1 fixed-income exchange, 1 government-owned or -controlled corporation, 11 insurance companies, and 1 savings bank (treasury).

OVERVIEW OF THE PHILIPPINES' SUSTAINABLE BOND MARKET

The Philippine sustainable bond market began to develop following the ASEAN Capital Markets Forum's introduction of the ASEAN Green Bond Standards in late 2017, followed by the ASEAN Social Bond Standards and ASEAN Sustainability Bond Standards in late 2018. The Securities and Exchange Commission (SEC) contributed significantly to the development of these standards, serving as co-chair of the ASEAN Capital Markets Forum's Sustainable Finance Working Group.

Subsequently, the SEC issued Memorandum Circular No. 12/2018 to establish guidelines for the issuance of green bonds in the Philippines that adhere to the ASEAN Green Bond Standards. Following that, the SEC issued Memorandum Circular No. 8/2019 establishing guidelines for the issuance of sustainability bonds and No. 9/2019 for social bond guidelines. These regulations fully implemented the ASEAN sustainable bond standards and acted as a catalyst for the development of the Philippine sustainable bond market.

In the Philippines, the total outstanding amount of green and sustainability bonds was USD4.2 billion as of December 2021, with all of these bonds having been issued by the private sector (**Figure 1**). Sustainability bonds were issued in January 2022 by two of the Philippines' largest banks: BDO Unibank

Figure 1: Sustainable Bonds Outstanding in the Philippine Market by Bond Type

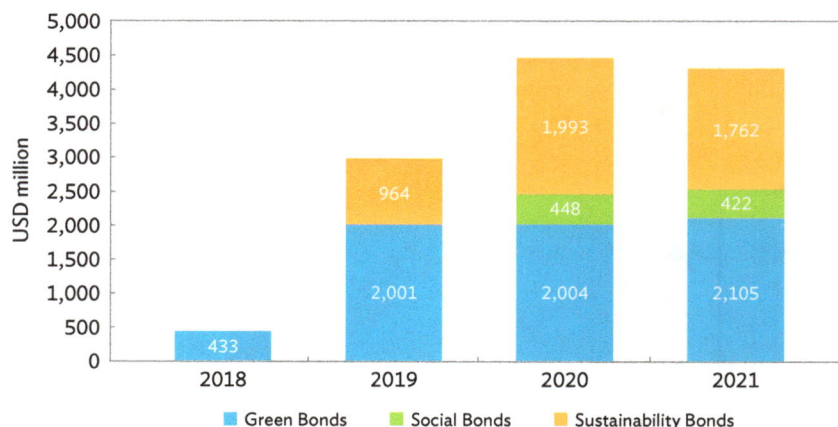

USD = United States dollar.
Note: All data as of 25 March 2022. Data were obtained using Bloomberg LP's SRCH function. The SRCH criteria include green bonds, social bonds, sustainability bonds, sustainability-linked bonds, and transition bonds.
Sources: *AsianBondsOnline* and Bloomberg LP.

worth PHP52.7 billion (USD1.0 billion) and Rizal Commercial Banking Corporation amounting to PHP14.7 billion (USD280 million).

Additionally, the majority of sustainable bonds issued in the Philippines have been green and sustainability bonds. Only the Bank of the Philippine Islands has issued a social bond in the domestic market (in August 2020). The issuance of its pioneering COVID-19 Action Response Bonds exceeded the initial target, as subscriptions for the offering reached PHP21.5 billion, more than seven times the initial planned issue size of PHP3.0 billion, triggering an expedited offer period closing for the country's first COVID-19 response bonds.[1] While financial institutions can issue social bonds to provide loans to micro, small, and medium-sized enterprises, the lack of interest in social bonds among corporate issuers can be attributed to two factors. First, the majority of social projects are deemed un-bankable, thus issuance of social bonds must be driven by the government or other public entities. Second, corporations prefer to issue sustainability bonds because the proceeds can be used to finance and/or refinance both green and social projects.

According to the SEC, the majority of sustainable bond issuers are financial institutions, followed by electric utilities and renewable energy firms (**Figures 2** and **4**). This reflects the Bangko Sentral ng Pilipinas' (BSP) policy of promoting environmental, social, and governance (ESG) integration and adoption among supervised financial institutions. In April 2020, the BSP issued Circular No. 1085 on the creation of a

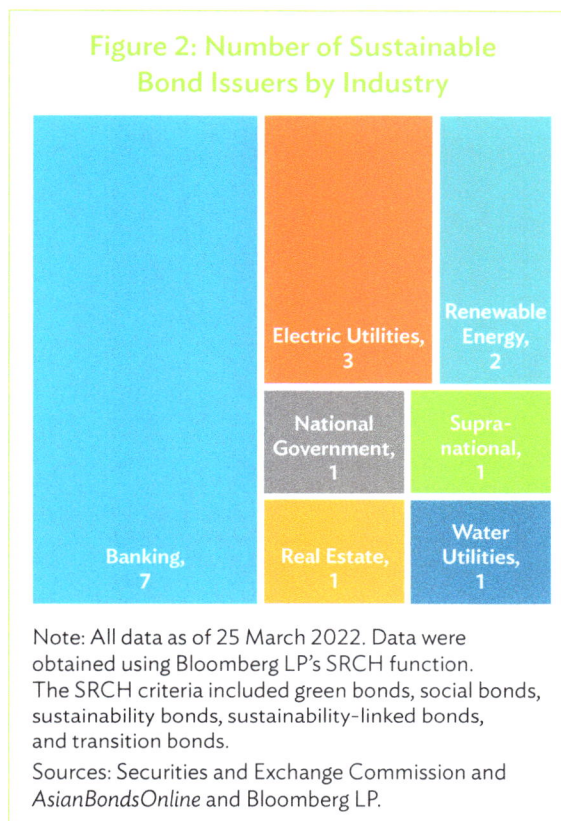

Figure 2: Number of Sustainable Bond Issuers by Industry

Note: All data as of 25 March 2022. Data were obtained using Bloomberg LP's SRCH function. The SRCH criteria included green bonds, social bonds, sustainability bonds, sustainability-linked bonds, and transition bonds.
Sources: Securities and Exchange Commission and *AsianBondsOnline* and Bloomberg LP.

sustainable finance framework encouraging supervised financial institutions to incorporate sustainability principles, including those covering environmental and social risk, into their corporate governance framework, risk management systems, and strategic objectives—in proportion to an institution's size, risk profile, and complexity of operations.[2]

In terms of currency, the majority of the sustainable bonds by Philippine companies have been issued in a foreign currency, led by the United States dollar and Swiss franc (**Figure 3**).

---

[1]   Bank of the Philippine Islands. 2020. BPI Raises 21.5 Billion from Pioneering-CARE-Bonds. Press release. 7 August.

[2]   Government of the Philippines, Bangko Sentral ng Pilipinas. 2020. BSP Circular 1085.

Figure 3: Issuance Currency of Sustainable Bonds Outstanding

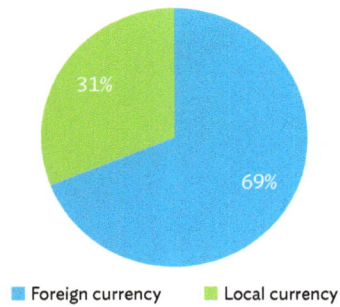

Note: All data as of 25 March 2022. Data were obtained using Bloomberg LP's SRCH function. The SRCH criteria included green bonds, social bonds, sustainability bonds, sustainability-linked bonds, and transition bonds.

Sources: Securities and Exchange Commission and *AsianBondsOnline* and Bloomberg LP.

Despite its rapid growth, particularly in 2019, as a result of the SEC's adoption of the ASEAN Green, Social, and Sustainability Bond Standards, the Philippines' sustainable bond market remains small in comparison to the country's overall LCY corporate bond market (**Figure 5**). As of December 2021, LCY sustainable bonds outstanding in the Philippines accounted for only 4.5% of the LCY corporate bond market.

Figure 4: Philippine Green, Social, and Sustainability Bond Issuances

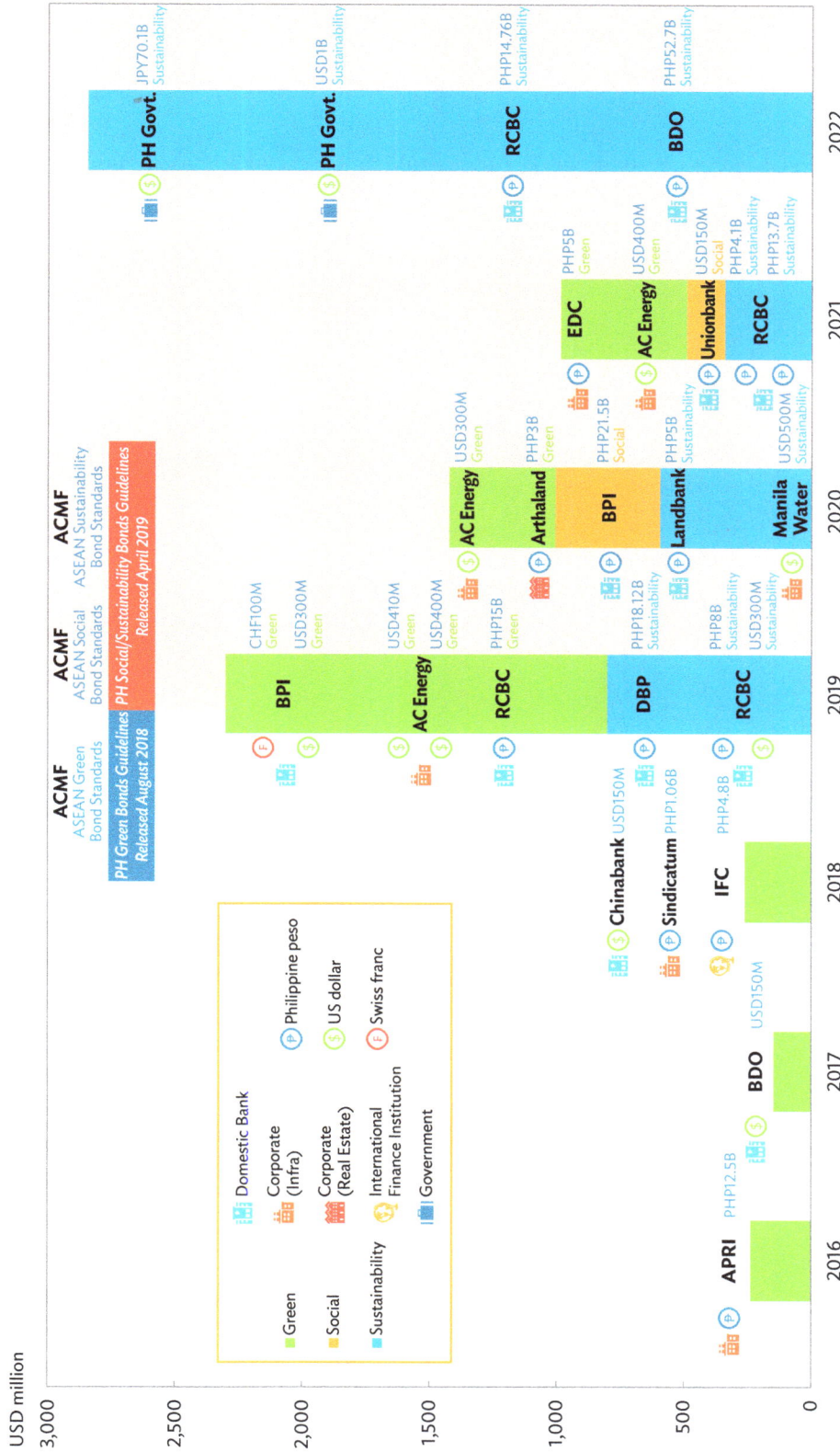

ACMF = ASEAN Capital Markets Forum, APRI = AP Renewables Inc., ASEAN = Association of Southeast Asian Nations, B = billion, BDO = Banco de Oro, BPI = Bank of the Philippine Islands, CHF = Swiss franc, DBP = Development Bank of the Philippines, EDC = Energy Development Corporation, IFC = International Finance Corporation, JPY = Japanese yen, M = million, PH = Philippines, PH Govt. = Philippine Government, PHP = Philippine peso, RCBC = Rizal Commercial Banking Corporation, US = United States, USD = United States dollar.

Source: Government of the Philippines, Securities and Exchange Commission. 2022. Sustainable Finance Market Update. 31 May.

Figure 5: Local Currency Sustainable Bonds Outstanding as a Share of the Local Currency Corporate Bond Market

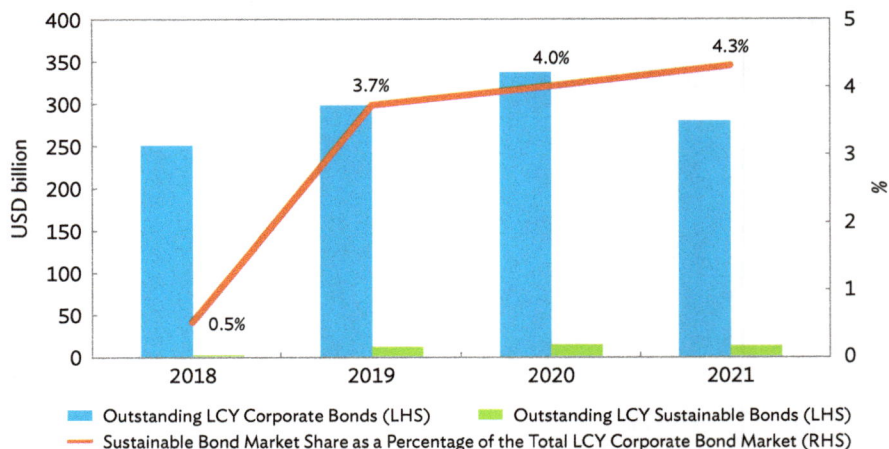

Legend:
- Outstanding LCY Corporate Bonds (LHS)
- Outstanding LCY Sustainable Bonds (LHS)
- Sustainable Bond Market Share as a Percentage of the Total LCY Corporate Bond Market (RHS)

LCY = local currency, LHS = left-hand side, RHS = right-hand side, USD = United States dollar.
Sources: *AsianBondsOnline* and Bloomberg LP.

RECENT INITIATIVES ON SUSTAINABLE FINANCE

The development of the sustainable finance market in the Philippines has been marked by the following milestones (**Figure 6**).

The sustainable finance market's development in the Philippines began in 2016 when AP Renewables, Inc., a subsidiary of Aboitiz Power Corporation, became the first issuer of a climate bond in Asia and the Pacific. ADB provided credit enhancement for a total of PHP10.7 billion (USD225.0 million) issued by AP Renewables, Inc., in addition to a direct loan of PHP1.8 billion (USD37.7 million) for its Tiwi–MakBan geothermal energy facilities. ADB provided credit enhancement in the form of a guarantee covering 75% of the bond's principal and interest. The Credit Guarantee and Investment Facility, a multilateral facility established by the governments of ASEAN+3 members and ADB to develop the region's bond markets, also participated in the risk-sharing arrangement.[3]

Subsequently, the SEC issued Memorandum Circular No. 12/2018 to establish guidelines for the issuance of green bonds in the Philippines that adhere to the ASEAN Green Bond Standards. Following that, the SEC issued Memorandum Circular No. 8/2019 establishing guidelines for the issuance of sustainability bonds and No. 9/2019 for social bond guidelines. Using these guidelines, the first green bond from the Philippines, under the ASEAN Green Bond Standards, was issued by Rizal Commercial Banking Corporation, which is also the first entity in the Philippines to have released a Green and Sustainability Bonds Impact Report.[4]

The SEC also instituted mandatory sustainability reporting through Memorandum Circular No. 4/2019 requiring all listed corporations to complete the following:[5]

(i) make sustainability reporting relevant and value adding for Philippine publicly listed companies (PLCs);

(ii) help PLCs to identify, evaluate, and manage their material economic, environmental, and social risks and opportunities;

(iii) help PLCs to assess and improve their nonfinancial performance across economic, environmental, and social aspects of their organization to optimize business operations, improve competitiveness, and achieve long-term success;

(iv) provide a mechanism that would allow PLCs to communicate with their stakeholders, including investors and potential investors; and

---

[3] ADB. 2016. ADB Backs First Climate Bond in Asia in Landmark USD225 Million Philippines Deal. News release. 29 February.

[4] ADB. 2020. Green Infrastructure Investment Opportunities: Philippines 2020 Report.

[5] Government of the Philippines, SEC. 2019. Memorandum Circular No. 4.

Figure 6: Timeline of Sustainable Finance Initiatives in the Philippines

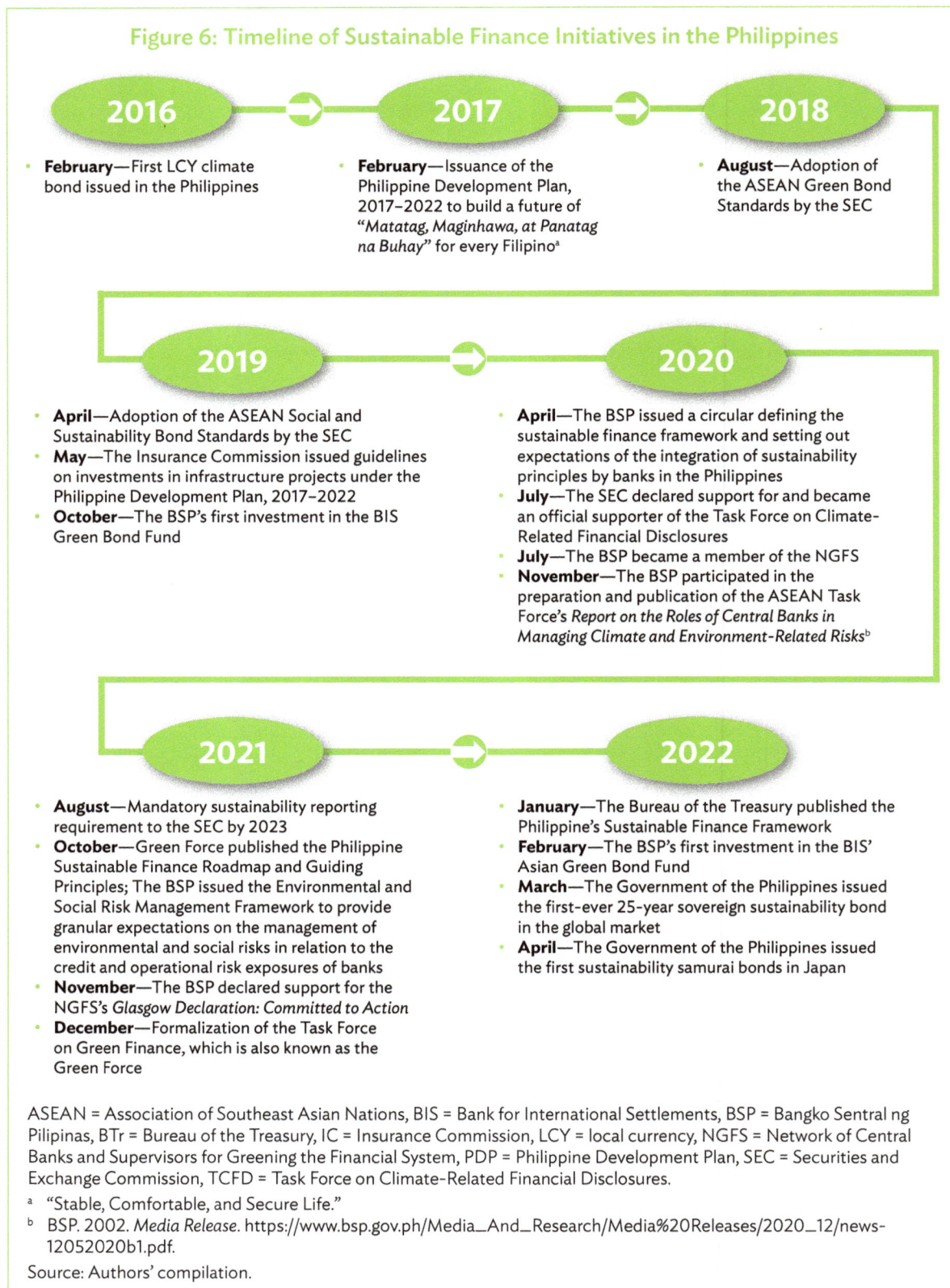

2016
- **February**—First LCY climate bond issued in the Philippines

2017
- **February**—Issuance of the Philippine Development Plan, 2017–2022 to build a future of *"Matatag, Maginhawa, at Panatag na Buhay"* for every Filipino[a]

2018
- **August**—Adoption of the ASEAN Green Bond Standards by the SEC

2019
- **April**—Adoption of the ASEAN Social and Sustainability Bond Standards by the SEC
- **May**—The Insurance Commission issued guidelines on investments in infrastructure projects under the Philippine Development Plan, 2017–2022
- **October**—The BSP's first investment in the BIS Green Bond Fund

2020
- **April**—The BSP issued a circular defining the sustainable finance framework and setting out expectations of the integration of sustainability principles by banks in the Philippines
- **July**—The SEC declared support for and became an official supporter of the Task Force on Climate-Related Financial Disclosures
- **July**—The BSP became a member of the NGFS
- **November**—The BSP participated in the preparation and publication of the ASEAN Task Force's *Report on the Roles of Central Banks in Managing Climate and Environment-Related Risks*[b]

2021
- **August**—Mandatory sustainability reporting requirement to the SEC by 2023
- **October**—Green Force published the Philippine Sustainable Finance Roadmap and Guiding Principles; The BSP issued the Environmental and Social Risk Management Framework to provide granular expectations on the management of environmental and social risks in relation to the credit and operational risk exposures of banks
- **November**—The BSP declared support for the NGFS's *Glasgow Declaration: Committed to Action*
- **December**—Formalization of the Task Force on Green Finance, which is also known as the Green Force

2022
- **January**—The Bureau of the Treasury published the Philippine's Sustainable Finance Framework
- **February**—The BSP's first investment in the BIS' Asian Green Bond Fund
- **March**—The Government of the Philippines issued the first-ever 25-year sovereign sustainability bond in the global market
- **April**—The Government of the Philippines issued the first sustainability samurai bonds in Japan

ASEAN = Association of Southeast Asian Nations, BIS = Bank for International Settlements, BSP = Bangko Sentral ng Pilipinas, BTr = Bureau of the Treasury, IC = Insurance Commission, LCY = local currency, NGFS = Network of Central Banks and Supervisors for Greening the Financial System, PDP = Philippine Development Plan, SEC = Securities and Exchange Commission, TCFD = Task Force on Climate-Related Financial Disclosures.

[a] "Stable, Comfortable, and Secure Life."
[b] BSP. 2002. *Media Release.* https://www.bsp.gov.ph/Media_And_Research/Media%20Releases/2020_12/news-12052020b1.pdf.

Source: Authors' compilation.

(v) enable PLCs to measure and monitor their contributions toward achieving universal targets of sustainability, such as the United Nations Sustainable Development Goals, as well as national policies and programs, such as AmBisyon Natin 2040.

In addition, the SEC declared support for and became an official supporter of the Task Force on Climate-Related Financial Disclosures in July 2020.[6]

At the same time, the BSP also became a member of the Network of Central Banks and Supervisors for Greening the Financial System (NGFS), a group of central banks and supervisors that, on a voluntary basis, exchange experiences, share best practices, contribute to the development of environment and climate risk management in the financial sector, and mobilize mainstream finance to support the transition toward a sustainable economy.[7] In November 2021, the BSP expressed its support for the NGFS' *Glasgow Declaration: Committed to Action,* which outlines the network's commitment to strengthening the financial system's resilience to climate-related and environmental risks and encourages the scaling up of financing flows necessary to support the transition to a sustainable economy.[8]

To demonstrate its commitment to green finance, the BSP was one of the region's first central banks to invest in the BIS' Asian Green Bond Fund. The fund invests in environmentally responsible projects throughout Asia and the Pacific and provides a platform for central banks to invest their reserves in high-quality green bonds that adhere to internationally recognized standards. The BSP made its first investment, totaling USD150 million, in 2019. The BSP has currently invested USD550 million under the BIS' Asian Green Bond Fund, which is part of the new BIS investment pool known as BISIP G3, and intends to continue doing so in the future.[9] According to the BIS, the new fund offers central banks, both in Asia and beyond, opportunities to invest in high-quality bonds issued by sovereigns, international financial institutions, and corporates that comply with strict international green standards. In addition, these bonds will help finance environmentally friendly projects in areas such as renewable energy production and energy efficiency in Asia and the Pacific.

As a regulator, the BSP is committed to setting an example by implementing the Sustainable Central Banking Program's initiatives to promote environmentally responsible and sustainable policies and practices. The Sustainable Central Banking Program exemplifies the BSP's critical roles as enabler, mobilizer, and doer in advocating for sustainability principles in the financial system.

The continued development of the green and sustainability bond markets was also supported by the Philippines' "whole of government" approach to sustainable and green finance with the establishment of the Interagency Task Force on Green Finance (Green Force) in 2019, led by the Department of Finance. The Task Force on Green Finance consists of 18 government agencies who developed a Philippine Sustainable Finance Roadmap, along with the Sustainable Finance Guiding Principles, which were introduced by members of the Green

---

[6] Task Force on Climate-Related Financial Disclosures Supporters.
[7] NGFS. Governance–Banque de France.
[8] NGFS. 2021. *Glasgow Declaration: Committed to Action.*
[9] Government of the Philippines, BSP. 2022. BSP Invests in BIS Asian Green Bond Fund in Sustainable Finance Push. Press release. 22 February.

Force on 29 October 2021.[10] Subsequently, the BSP issued Circular Letter No. CL-2022-011 to direct the release of the roadmap and guiding principles among licensed financial institutions in the Philippines. According to the circular, the roadmap sets out a comprehensive approach that will serve as the foundation for effective strategies to facilitate the mainstreaming of sustainable finance in the country, while the guiding principles establish a common understanding among various stakeholders of the economic activities considered sustainable.[11] Moreover, the key plans for the development of sustainable finance include the following:

(i)   integrating sustainability considerations into macroeconomic policies and regulations;
(ii) embedding sustainability into the risk management of the banking, insurance, and asset management sectors;
(iii) encouraging sustainability and climate-related disclosures;
(iv) improving the sustainable finance definition and creation of a principles-based taxonomy;
(v)   establishing a sustainable pipeline database, both for public and private sector projects; and
(vi) joining international initiatives on sustainable finance.

Meanwhile, the Bureau of the Treasury established the country's Sustainable Finance Framework in January 2022 to support its sustainability initiatives, paving the way for the country to issue green, social, and sustainability bonds, loans, and other debt instruments in international capital markets.[12] The Philippines became the latest ASEAN country to issue its first-ever sovereign sustainability bond with the issuance of the country's 25-year sustainability dollar global bond in March 2022.[13] The 25-year global bond was issued under the Philippines' Sustainable Finance Framework and marks the country's debut ESG global bond offering. In April 2022, the Philippines also issued JPY70.1 billion worth of 5-, 7-, 10-, and 20-year sustainability samurai bonds in Japan with an ESG label across all four tranches.[14]

Moreover, the Philippines' Insurance Commission advocates for the adoption of sound ESG practices by insurance companies and the industry as a whole. The Insurance Commission, along with the Philippine Insurers and Reinsurers Association and the Philippine Life Insurance Association, supports the United Nations Environment Programme Finance Initiative's Principles for Sustainable Insurance, which serve as a global framework for the insurance industry to address ESG risks and opportunities.

In relation to this, the Insurance Commission issued Circular Letter No. 2019-19 to encourage insurance and professional reinsurance companies to invest in various infrastructure projects—particularly in the areas of environmental and solid waste management, and climate change mitigation and adaptation infrastructure projects—under

10   Government of the Philippines, Department of Finance. 2021. Green Force Members, Multilateral Agencies Support Sustainable Finance Roadmap. News release. 29 October.

11   Government of the Philippines, BSP. 2021. Circular Letter No. CL-2022-011 on the Philippine Sustainable Finance Roadmap and Guiding Principles.

12   Government of the Philippines, Bureau of the Treasury. 2022. Republic of the Philippines Sustainability Framework.

13   Government of the Philippines, Bureau of the Treasury. 2022. Republic of the Philippines Prices 5-Year, 10.5-Year, and Debut 25-Year Sustainability Dollar Global Bonds. Press release.

14   Government of the Philippines, Bureau of the Treasury. 2022. The Republic of the Philippines Launches Its First Sustainability Samurai Bond in Japan. Press release.

the Philippine Development Plan, 2017–2022, which aims to promote inclusive growth, a resilient society, and responsible investing through ESG finance products in the insurance industry.[15] In addition, the Insurance Commission is currently building its ESG capacities, including

through international affiliations such as with the ASEAN Taxonomy Board and ASEAN Working Committee on Capital Market Development.

The Philippine's sustainable finance ecosystem is depicted in Figure 7.

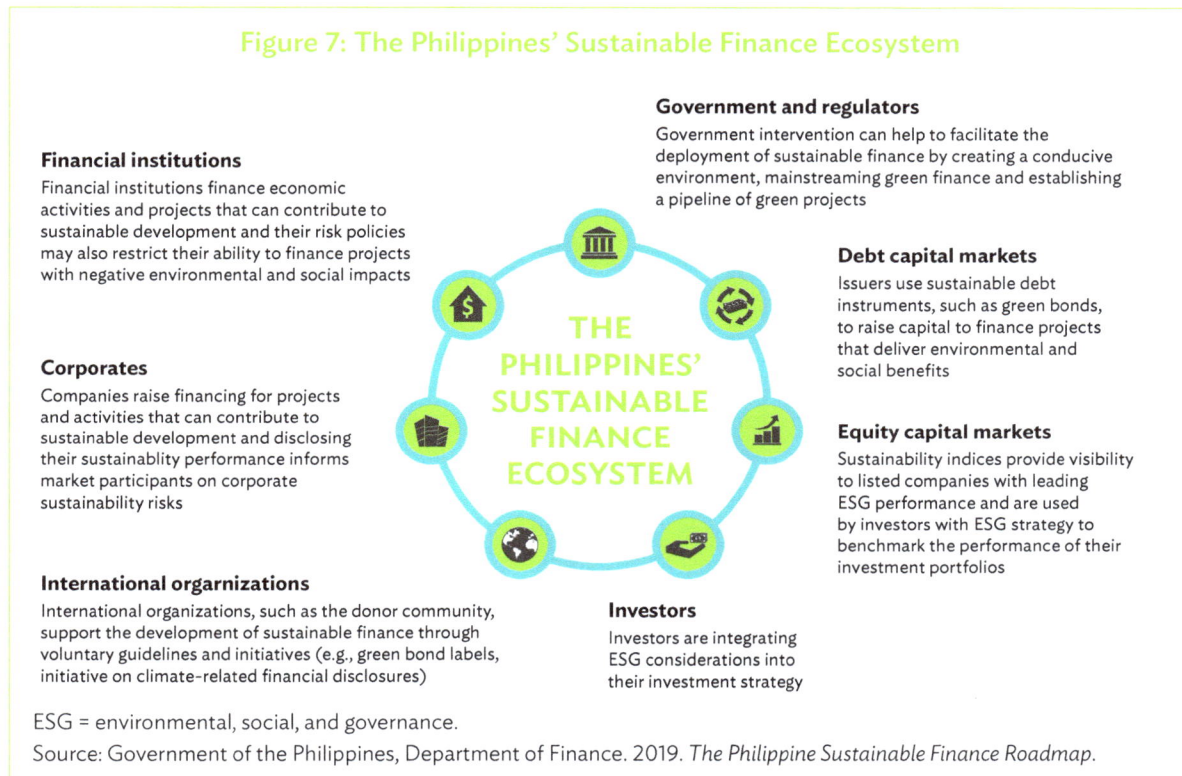

Figure 7: The Philippines' Sustainable Finance Ecosystem

Financial institutions
Financial institutions finance economic activities and projects that can contribute to sustainable development and their risk policies may also restrict their ability to finance projects with negative environmental and social impacts

Corporates
Companies raise financing for projects and activities that can contribute to sustainable development and disclosing their sustainablity performance informs market participants on corporate sustainability risks

International orgarnizations
International organizations, such as the donor community, support the development of sustainable finance through voluntary guidelines and initiatives (e.g., green bond labels, initiative on climate-related financial disclosures)

Government and regulators
Government intervention can help to facilitate the deployment of sustainable finance by creating a conducive environment, mainstreaming green finance and establishing a pipeline of green projects

Debt capital markets
Issuers use sustainable debt instruments, such as green bonds, to raise capital to finance projects that deliver environmental and social benefits

Equity capital markets
Sustainability indices provide visibility to listed companies with leading ESG performance and are used by investors with ESG strategy to benchmark the performance of their investment portfolios

Investors
Investors are integrating ESG considerations into their investment strategy

ESG = environmental, social, and governance.
Source: Government of the Philippines, Department of Finance. 2019. *The Philippine Sustainable Finance Roadmap.*

[15] Government of the Philippines, Insurance Commission. 2019. Circular No. 2019-19.

SURVEY RESULTS

The survey was conducted in January 2022 among local institutional investors—including fund managers, financial institutions, and insurance companies—and local underwriters and advisors. A summary of the survey's findings is given below.

Institutional Investors

The survey began by asking respondents about their firms' interest and/or current investment in green financial instruments. The majority of respondents indicated exploring green financial instruments but also having limited awareness and resources, while some others are interested and developing an action plan (**Figure 8**). Those exploring green investments are mostly insurance companies. Meanwhile, around 10% of the respondents indicated a lack of interest in green bonds due to market instability, lack of knowledge, risk appetite, preference for investments in equity securities only, and pandemic-related effects on capital. One fixed-income exchange respondent reported that being market operators, they support the issuance and listing of green, social, and sustainability bonds, and are developing supplemental disclosure requirements for issuers of such bonds.

The fact that the majority of respondents are exploring green bonds, but have limited awareness and resources, accounts for green bonds comprising less than 5% of their aggregate portfolios. One respondent, a brokerage firm

Figure 8: Interest in Investing in Green Bonds

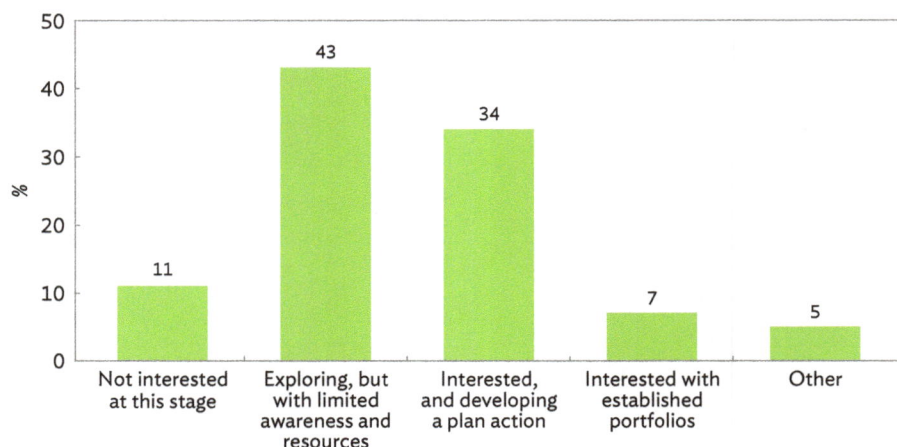

Source: Authors' compilation based on survey results.

(proprietary trading), indicated that green investments accounted for between 11% and 20% of its portfolio, while the other, an insurance company, indicated investments of between 6% and 10%.

When asked about ticket size, 67% of respondents indicated a preference for investments of less than USD10 million, while 13% indicated a willingness to invest up to USD50 million per transaction (**Figure 9**). Only 5% of respondents indicated more than USD100 million as investment preference. Around 6% of respondents mentioned flexibility and consideration on a case-by-case basis depending on the client's requirement, risk appetite, and regulatory ceiling. No responses were received for investments between >USD50 million and USD100 million.

In terms of sector preference, renewable energy (32%), water management (13%), and energy efficiency (10%) are the top sectors in terms of comprising a share of respondents' investment portfolios (**Figure 10**). Meanwhile, 23% of respondents have no exposure to green investments, while only 7% of respondents

have invested in waste management and the circular economy.

When respondents were asked their primary reasons for investing in green bonds, the majority of investors believed that the opportunity to embed the Sustainable Development Goals in their investment strategy is critical (**Figure 11**). This could also contribute to the organization's public image. Additionally, respondents indicated that clear regulatory requirements being established by the relevant regulators

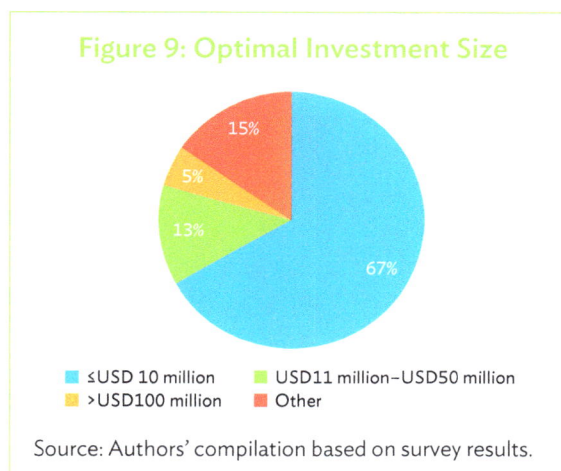

Figure 9: Optimal Investment Size

Legend: ≤USD 10 million; USD11 million–USD50 million; >USD100 million; Other

Source: Authors' compilation based on survey results.

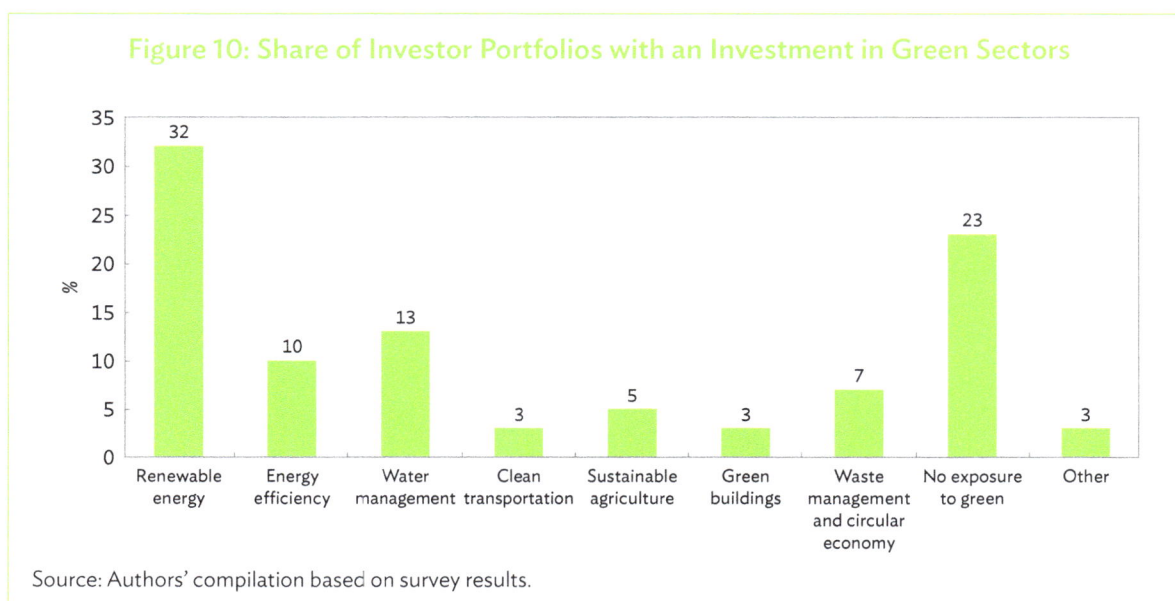

Figure 10: Share of Investor Portfolios with an Investment in Green Sectors

Values: Renewable energy 32; Energy efficiency 10; Water management 13; Clean transportation 3; Sustainable agriculture 5; Green buildings 3; Waste management and circular economy 7; No exposure to green 23; Other 3

Source: Authors' compilation based on survey results.

Figure 11: Key Motivations for Investing in Green Bonds

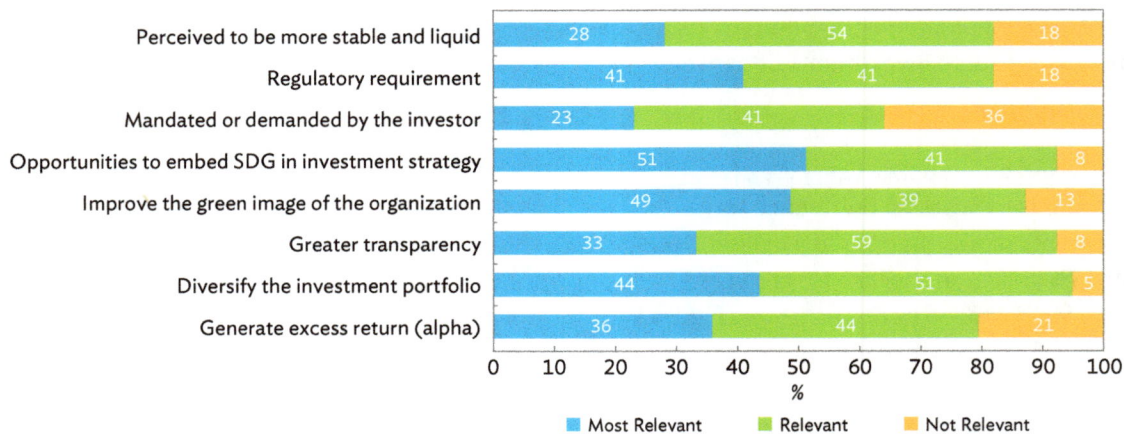

Motivation	Most Relevant	Relevant	Not Relevant
Perceived to be more stable and liquid	28	54	18
Regulatory requirement	41	41	18
Mandated or demanded by the investor	23	41	36
Opportunities to embed SDG in investment strategy	51	41	8
Improve the green image of the organization	49	39	13
Greater transparency	33	59	8
Diversify the investment portfolio	44	51	5
Generate excess return (alpha)	36	44	21

SDG = Sustainable Development Goal.
Source: Authors' compilation based on survey results.

would be the primary factor motivating them to invest in green bonds. Meanwhile, nearly 95% of respondents believed that investing in green bonds would increase their portfolio diversification. Also, greater transparency is a substantial consideration for investing in green bonds.

To help ADB and local regulators support the development of green bond markets, investors were asked to identify any major obstacles to investing in green bonds (**Figure 12**). Around 25% of respondents stated that the primary impediment is a lack of understanding of the clear benefits of green bonds as opposed to

Figure 12: Main Obstacles Preventing Investors from Investing in Green Bonds

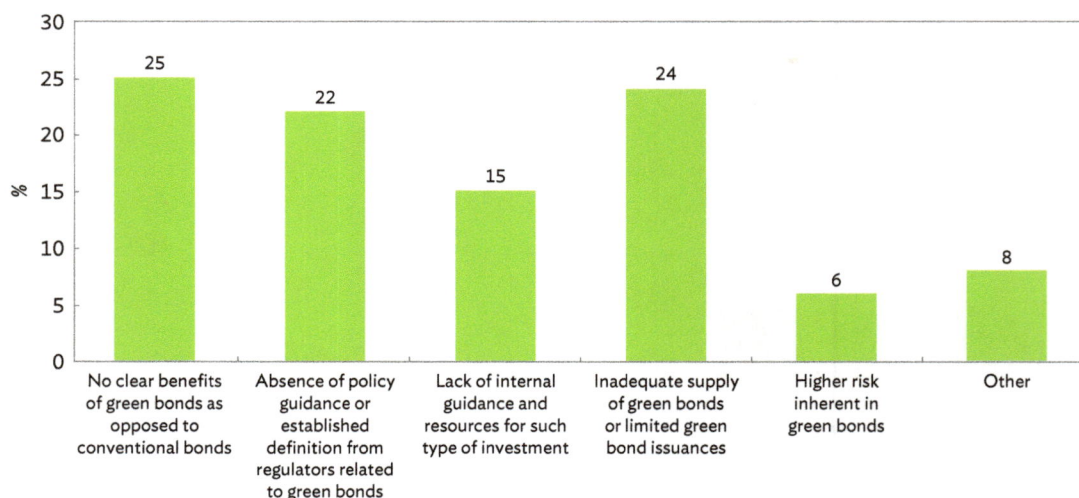

Obstacle	%
No clear benefits of green bonds as opposed to conventional bonds	25
Absence of policy guidance or established definition from regulators related to green bonds	22
Lack of internal guidance and resources for such type of investment	15
Inadequate supply of green bonds or limited green bond issuances	24
Higher risk inherent in green bonds	6
Other	8

Source: Authors' compilation based on survey results.

conventional bonds. Additionally, 24% of respondents indicated that an inadequate supply of green bonds or limited green bond issuance was one of the key inhibiting factors, while nearly 22% indicated that the absence of regulatory guidance on green bonds is also an impediment. One respondent mentioned still being in the learning stage in this field.

When investing in green bonds, respondents give the highest prioritization to valuation and pricing, followed by a company's profile (**Figure 13**). The third priority is the ESG impact of the bond and how the issuer intends to use the proceeds to benefit the environment. One respondent indicated that the Philippine green bond market is still a sunrise industry; hence, development of a regulatory framework, risk assessment and monitoring, and internal skill expertise are needed. Moreover, the reliance on external review is a significant consideration too.

To address these issues, respondents were requested to select up to three options that they felt could encourage the growth of the

Philippines' green bond market. Nearly 21% of respondents recommended that the government implement tax incentives and/or subsidies to entice investors to hold more green bonds (**Figure 14**). Meanwhile, over 19% of respondents indicated that regulatory support and guidance, as well as a legal requirement to allocate a certain portion of portfolios to green assets, would significantly facilitate investors' decisions in green investments. In effect, this would promote the right of the people to a balanced and healthful ecology in accord with the rhythm and harmony of nature, as outlined in the Philippine Constitution.

As previously stated, investors believe that the domestic supply of green bonds issued in the Philippines is insufficient to meet their demand. The survey investigated which types of issuers of green bonds respondents are interested in. Local institutional investors indicated that they are most interested in sovereign issuances, followed by financial institutions and development banks (**Figure 15**). The recently established Sustainable Finance Framework to support the country's sustainability

Figure 13: Key Considerations for Investing in Green Bonds

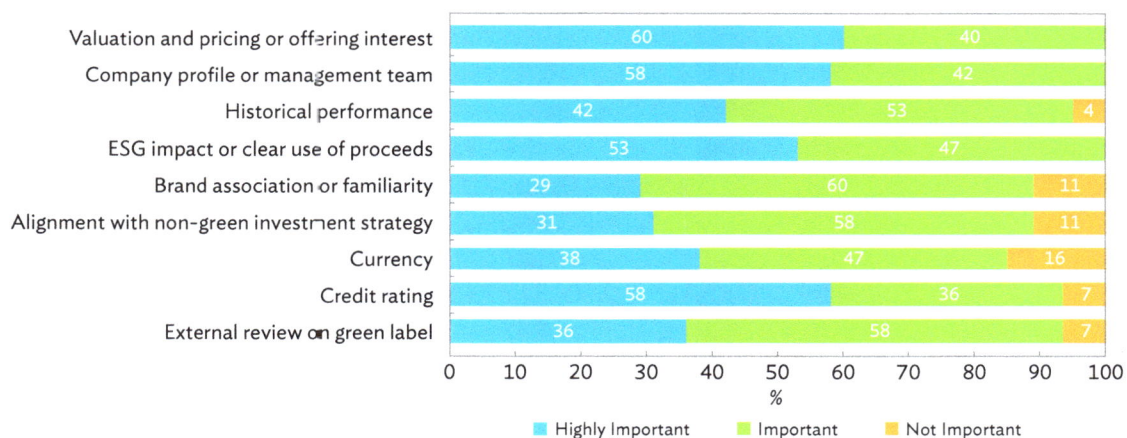

ESG = environmental, social, and governance.
Source: Authors' compilation based on survey results.

Figure 14: Policy Mechanisms That Would Increase Green Bond Investments

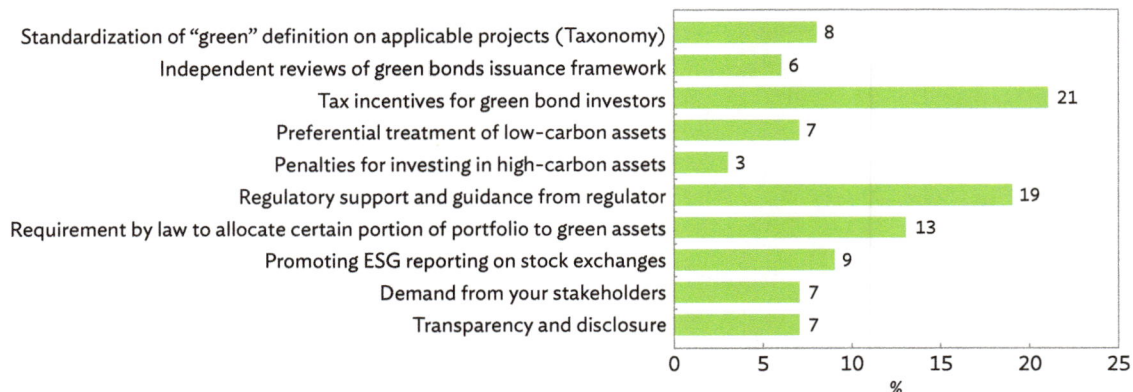

Policy Mechanism	%
Standardization of "green" definition on applicable projects (Taxonomy)	8
Independent reviews of green bonds issuance framework	6
Tax incentives for green bond investors	21
Preferential treatment of low-carbon assets	7
Penalties for investing in high-carbon assets	3
Regulatory support and guidance from regulator	19
Requirement by law to allocate certain portion of portfolio to green assets	13
Promoting ESG reporting on stock exchanges	9
Demand from your stakeholders	7
Transparency and disclosure	7

ESG = environmental, social, and governance.
Source: Authors' compilation based on survey results.

Figure 15: Level of Local Investor Interest by Issuer Type

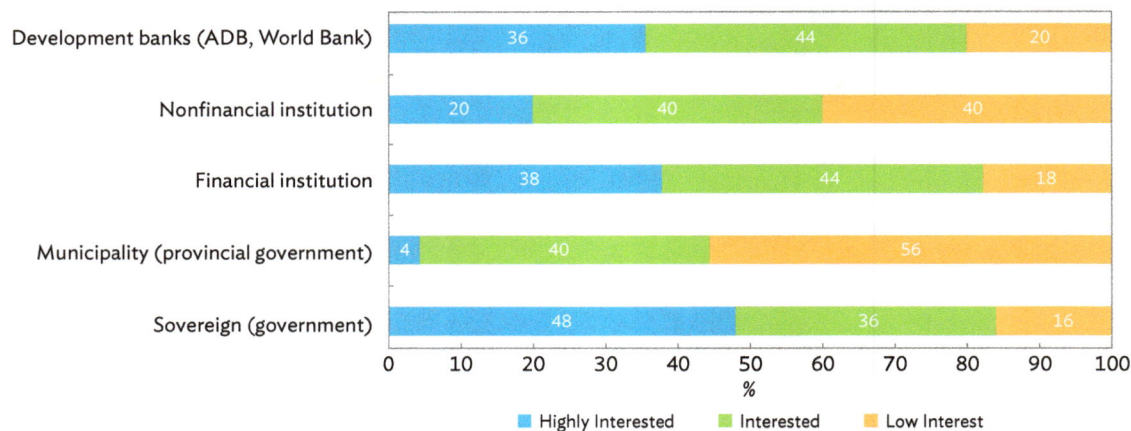

Issuer Type	Highly Interested	Interested	Low Interest
Development banks (ADB, World Bank)	36	44	20
Nonfinancial institution	20	40	40
Financial institution	38	44	18
Municipality (provincial government)	4	40	56
Sovereign (government)	48	36	16

ADB = Asian Development Bank.
Source: Authors' compilation based on survey results.

initiative would enable the Government of the Philippines to raise green, social, or sustainability bonds, loans, and other debt instruments in international capital markets and provide investors with additional investment opportunities. The framework would ensure transparency and disclosure on the use of proceeds in line with international best practices. In terms of sectors, over 29% of respondents believed that renewable energy offers the

greatest investment potential in the Philippines (**Figure 16**). This finding is consistent with the sector breakdown of respondents' current portfolios of green assets.

On policy options to develop a green bond market, all respondents emphasized the critical importance of policy clarity from the government and regulators, tax incentives or subsidies for green bond issuers or investors, as well as a clear

Figure 16: Sectors with Most Potential for Green Bond Investments

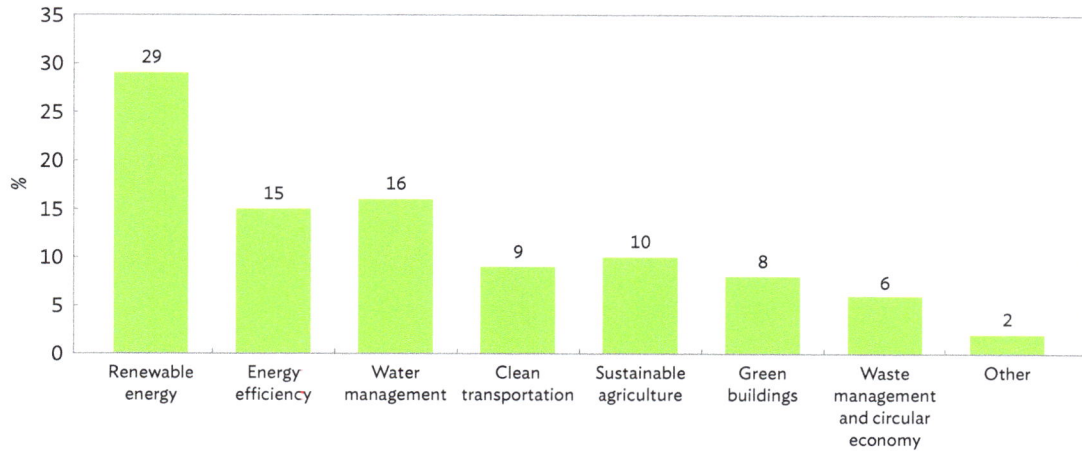

Renewable energy 29, Energy efficiency 15, Water management 16, Clean transportation 9, Sustainable agriculture 10, Green buildings 8, Waste management and circular economy 6, Other 2

Source: Authors' compilation based on survey results.

"green" definition. Nearly 58% of respondents believed these to be the most relevant factors. Among the objectives of this policy guidance are the establishment of clear guidelines for green bond issuance procedures, enhancement of the reporting framework, and disclosure of green bonds.

Around 60% of respondents indicated that tax incentives and subsidies for green bond

issuers were very relevant. This was followed by an increased pipeline of eligible projects for green bonds issuance and policy clarity from governments and regulators (**Figure 17**). Additionally, this would provide encouragement to investors and issuers alike. All respondents recognized the need for policy clarity from governments and regulators for the green bond market to further develop in the Philippines. Furthermore, respondents viewed that making

Figure 17: Policy Options for Green Bond Market Development

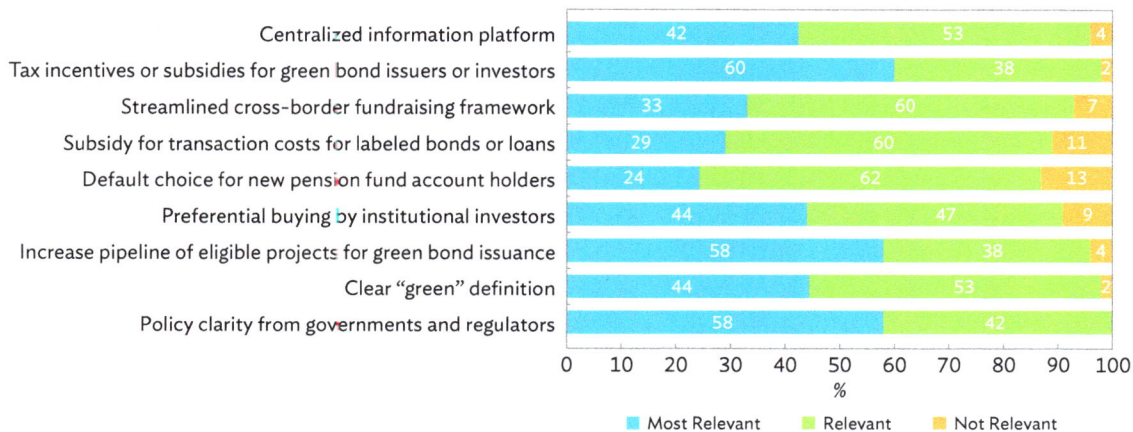

Policy	Most Relevant	Relevant	Not Relevant
Centralized information platform	42	53	4
Tax incentives or subsidies for green bond issuers or investors	60	38	2
Streamlined cross-border fundraising framework	33	60	7
Subsidy for transaction costs for labeled bonds or loans	29	60	11
Default choice for new pension fund account holders	24	62	13
Preferential buying by institutional investors	44	47	9
Increase pipeline of eligible projects for green bond issuance	58	38	4
Clear "green" definition	44	53	2
Policy clarity from governments and regulators	58	42	

Source: Authors' compilation based on survey results.

green bonds the default choice for new pension fund account holders is also important.

Regarding capacity development, respondents unanimously agreed that both investors and the asset management and deal teams within investment banks and securities firms require additional training (**Figure 18**). Additionally, board members of state-owned banks and state-owned enterprises should be trained to gain a better understanding of green bonds.

This would help increase the supply of green bonds to meet investor demand.

The majority of respondents intend to invest in the region (**Figure 19**). Among this group, Singapore, Indonesia, Thailand, and Viet Nam are the preferred investment destinations. When asked about the underlying currency, around 40% of respondents prefer investments denominated in hard currencies such as the United States dollar, euro, and yen (**Figure 20**).

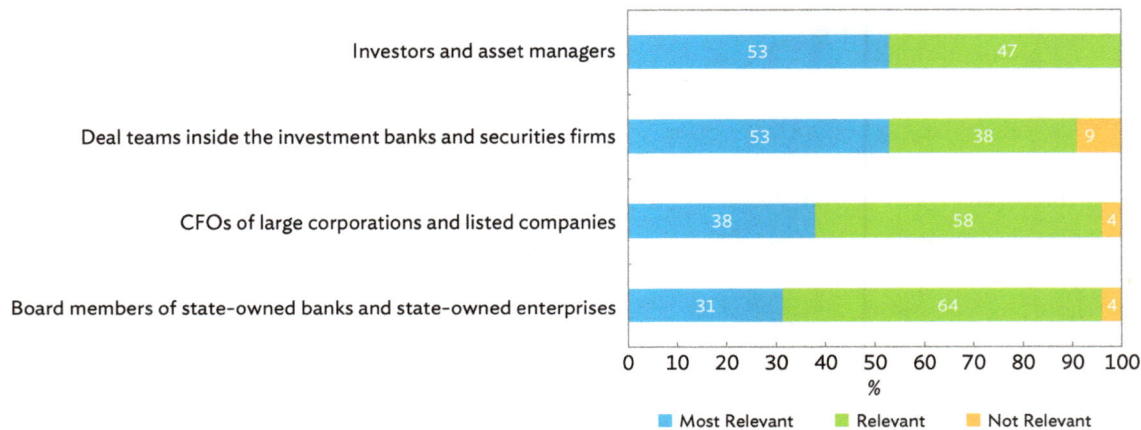

Figure 18: Capacity Building—Who Should Be Trained?

CFO = chief financial officer.
Source: Authors' compilation based on survey results.

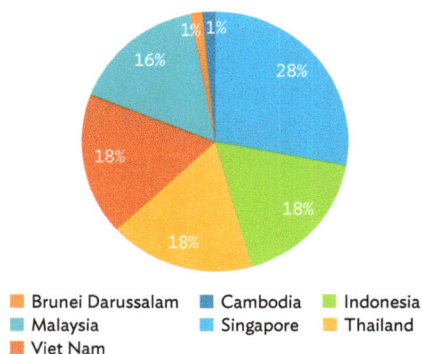

Figure 19: Investor Interest in Regional Investment

Source: Authors' compilation based on survey results.

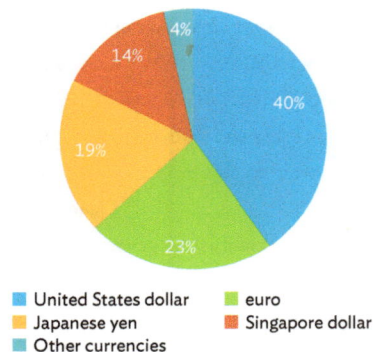

Figure 20: Preferred Underlying Currencies

Source: Authors' compilation based on survey results.

Advisors and Underwriters

This section examines the interest of potential green bond issuers, the most promising economic sectors, and the various types of potential issuers based on responses from local advisors and underwriters.

The survey began by asking whether respondents' clients are interested in issuing green bonds. Responses showed that their clients are generally interested in and are developing plans for green bond issuance. Several clients have already issued green bonds, while others are exploring the possibility but lack the necessary resources and awareness. This may be an area where development partners such as ADB can assist interested entities with technical assistance and capacity building (**Figure 21**).

In terms of issuance size, almost 67% of respondents indicated that the optimal issuance size for green financial instruments is greater than USD100 million, while 33% of surveyed underwriters felt that the optimal deal size should be between USD11 million

and USD50 million (**Figure 22**). This finding is in contrast with institutional investors' preference for investments of less than USD10 million, with only 5% of institutional investor respondents indicating more than USD100 million as an investment preference. All respondents mentioned that their clients prefer issuance of green bonds in Philippine peso (**Figure 23**).

In terms of sectors, all respondents agreed that renewable energy, green buildings, water management, and sustainable agriculture would present the greatest opportunities for

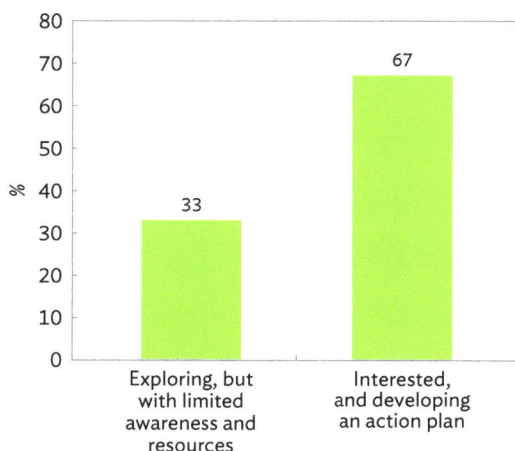

Figure 22: Optimal Issuance Size

- USD11 million–USD50 million (33%)
- USD51 million–USD100 million (67%)

Source: Authors' compilation based on survey results.

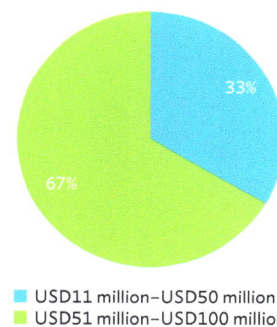

Figure 21: Interest in Issuing Green Bonds

Exploring, but with limited awareness and resources: 33
Interested, and developing an action plan: 67

Source: Authors' compilation based on survey results.

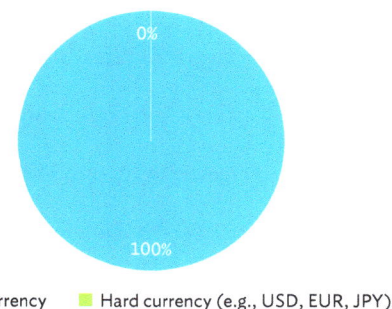

Figure 23: Preferred Currency Denomination

- Local currency (100%)
- Hard currency (e.g., USD, EUR, JPY) (0%)

EUR = euro, JPY = Japanese yen, USD = United States dollar.
Source: Authors' compilation based on survey results.

green bond issuance in the Philippine market over the next 3 years (**Figure 24**). This finding is consistent with institutional investors' perspectives and the current composition of their green asset portfolios.

When asked why clients should issue green bonds, all respondents believe that it could

result in an opportunity to attract new investors. Around 67% of respondents believed this was among the most compelling reasons for companies to issue green bonds, while 33% believed it was a valid reason (**Figure 25**). Additionally, all respondents believed increasing the quality of corporate disclosure and improving the green image of the organization would be a

Figure 24: Most Promising Sectors for Green Bonds Issuance

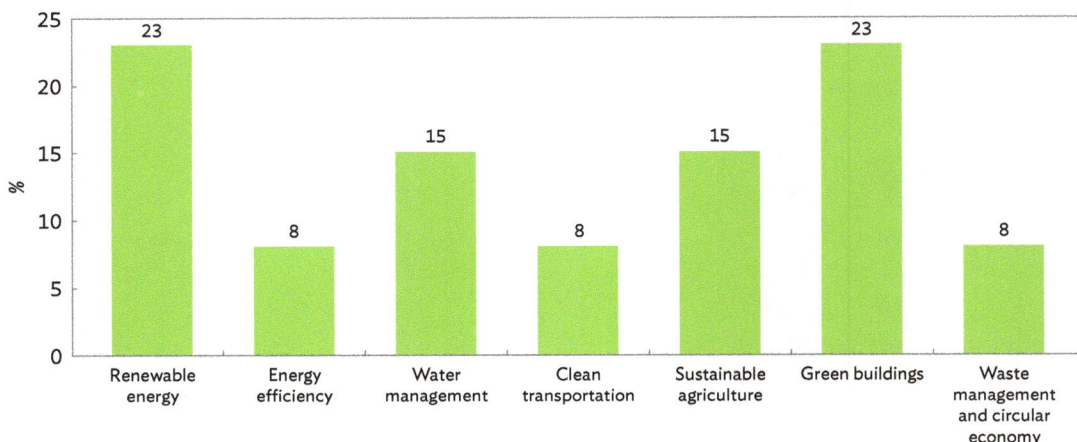

Source: Authors' compilation based on survey results.

Figure 25: Key Motivations for Issuing Green Bonds

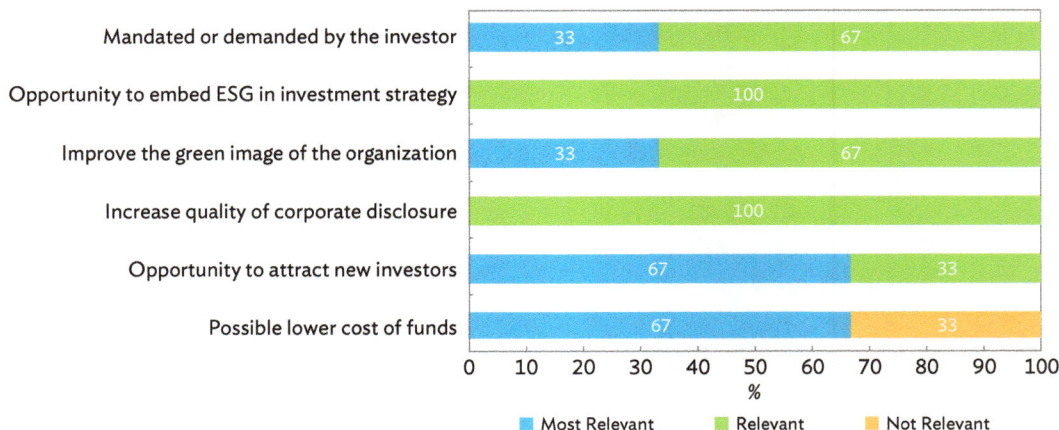

ESG = environmental, social, and governance.
Source: Authors' compilation based on survey results.

key driver for issuers to incorporate ESG as part of their corporate DNA.

Concerning market development, 40% of respondents identified the lack of knowledge or awareness of green bonds as the main impediment to their clients issuing green bonds. Another 40% believed it was green bonds' benefits being unclear compared with conventional bonds (**Figure 26**). Finally, 20% view the lack of eligible project pipelines as the main obstacle preventing issuance.

Respondents were then asked to identify the primary policy mechanisms that would increase green bond issuance in the Philippines. The largest share of respondents (30%) indicated that tax incentives or subsidies for green bond issuers would be the primary factor to consider, followed by the demand from investors (20%) (**Figure 27**).

When asked about potential investors, nearly 67% of respondents believed that development partners such as ADB and asset managers could significantly contribute to the development of the local green bond market by investing in green

bonds issued by their clients. All respondents agreed that insurance companies and financial institutions could invest in green bonds, with nearly 70% believing that insurance companies could play a significant role in facilitating the issuance of longer-term debt. Additionally, respondents believed that if retail investors

Figure 26: Main Obstacles Preventing Issuers from Investing in Green Bonds

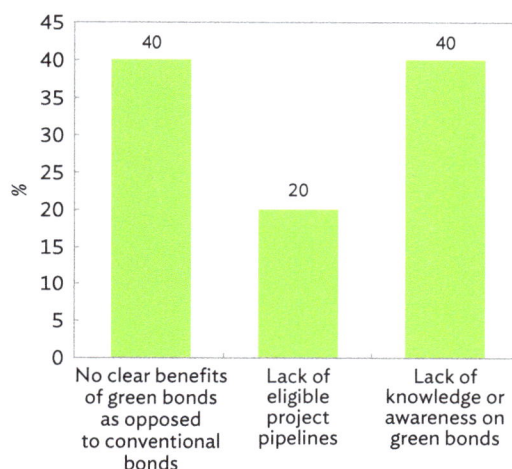

Source: Authors' compilation based on survey results.

Figure 27: Key Drivers for Green Bonds Issuance

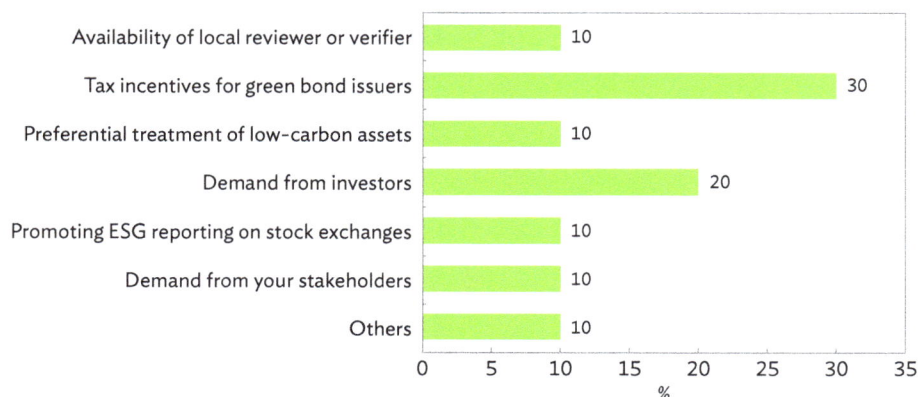

ESG = environmental, social, and governance.
Source: Authors' compilation based on survey results.

gained a better understanding of ESG investing, they would be able to invest in green bonds via pension and social security funds, and that these funds could become mainstream investors (**Figure 28**).

Similar to institutional investors, underwriters and advisors believe that tax incentives for

issuers and investors, as well as preferential purchasing from central banks, pension funds, and insurance companies, and the clear definition of green projects, are necessary to further develop the Philippines' green bond market (**Figure 29**). More than 67% of respondents believed that a centralized information platform and policy clarity from

---

Figure 28: Preferred Investors in Green Bonds

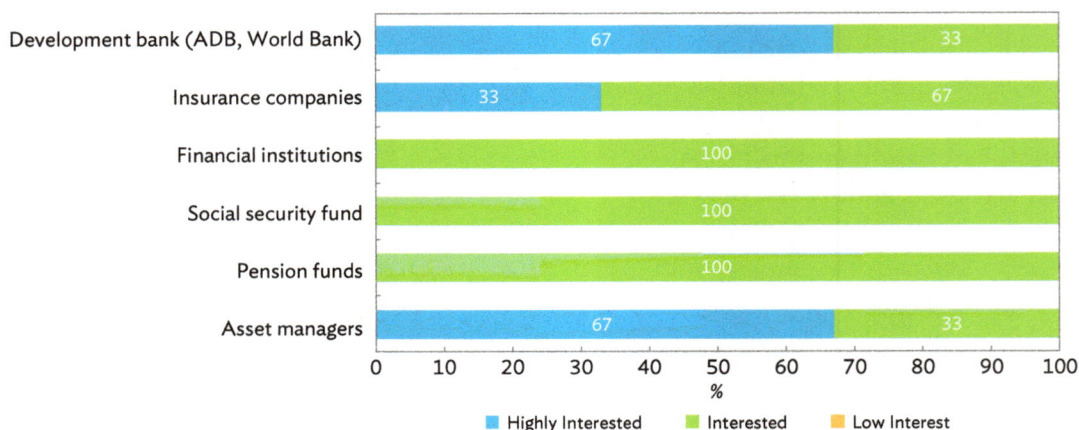

Category	Highly Interested	Interested
Development bank (ADB, World Bank)	67	33
Insurance companies	33	67
Financial institutions		100
Social security fund		100
Pension funds		100
Asset managers	67	33

Legend: ■ Highly Interested ■ Interested ■ Low Interest

ADB = Asian Development Bank.
Source: Authors' compilation based on survey results.

Figure 29: Policy Relevance for the Green Bond Market's Development

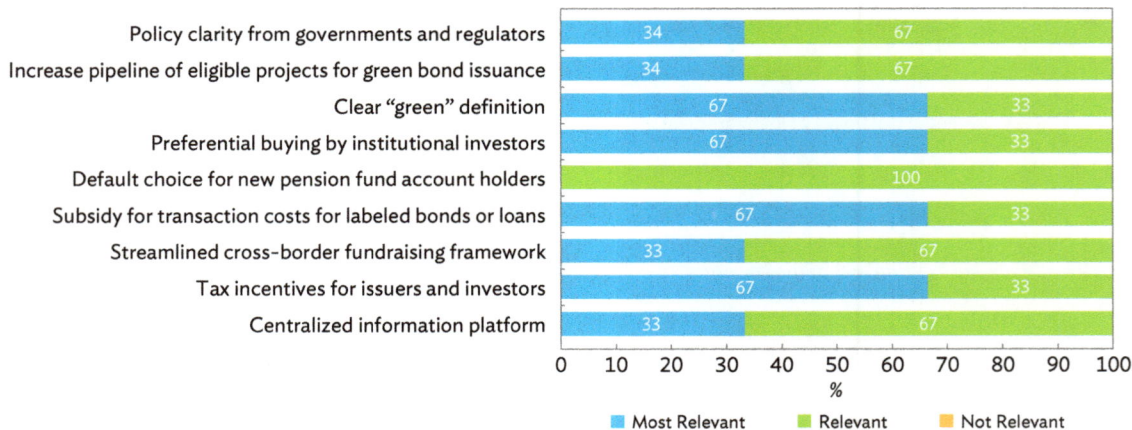

Category	Most Relevant	Relevant
Policy clarity from governments and regulators	34	67
Increase pipeline of eligible projects for green bond issuance	34	67
Clear "green" definition	67	33
Preferential buying by institutional investors	67	33
Default choice for new pension fund account holders		100
Subsidy for transaction costs for labeled bonds or loans	67	33
Streamlined cross-border fundraising framework	33	67
Tax incentives for issuers and investors	67	33
Centralized information platform	33	67

Legend: ■ Most Relevant ■ Relevant ■ Not Relevant

Source: Authors' compilation based on survey results.

governments and regulators are equally relevant for green bond development. Underwriters and advisors believed that making green bonds the default choice for new pension fund account holders is also important.

In terms of capacity building, all respondents believe that institutional investors, the chief finance officers of large corporations and listed companies, and board members of state-owned banks and enterprises can benefit from training to better understand green bonds and why they should include them in their financing strategy (**Figure 30**). Indeed, 67% of respondents believed that training for these three groups of stakeholders is of critical importance. All respondents agreed that deal teams within investment banks and, to a lesser extent, underwriters require training as well.

Figure 30: Capacity Building—Who Should Be Trained?

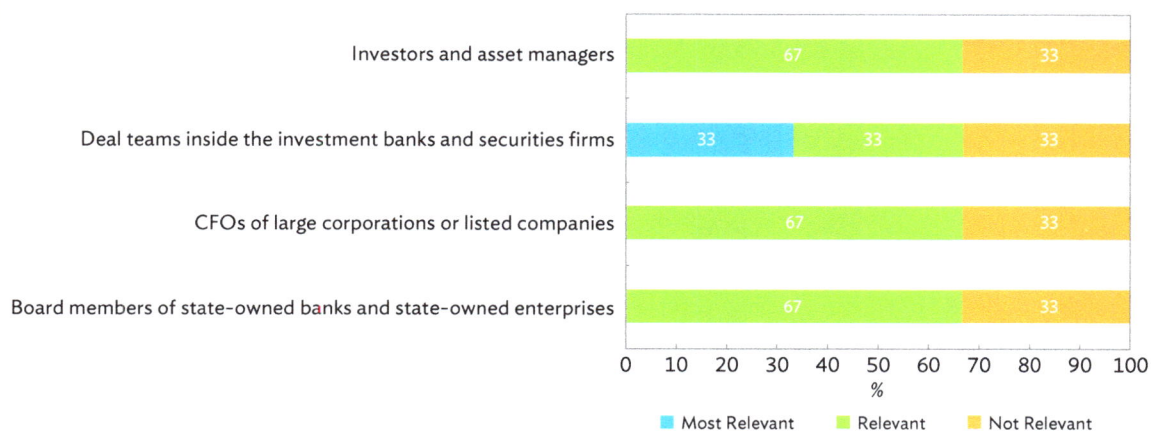

CFO = chief financial officer.
Source: Authors' compilation based on survey results.

WHAT ADB CAN DO TO HELP

Lastly, respondents identified several ways in which ADB could assist the Philippine green bond market's development. These beneficial recommendations can be classified as follows.

As a Knowledge Partner

ADB could provide knowledge support to relevant stakeholders in the Philippines, including potential issuers, capital market intermediaries, institutional investors, and the general public **(Box 1)**.

ADB could promote global best practices, methodologies, tools, and disclosure standards within the public and private sectors through advisory and knowledge support in government roadmaps and industry forums for technology sharing. Moreover, ADB could standardize reporting and disclosure requirements to limit subjectivity in ESG rating.

Partnership with regulatory agencies to promote the green bond market is recommended.

As an Investor

ADB can also provide subsidies for the registration and certification processes of green bond issuances.

One respondent explained that aside from supporting the capital market's development, ADB can also provide credit and tenor enhancements to issuers of green bonds.

Furthermore, a respondent suggested that ADB could provide financing support and technical assistance to strategic sectors, industries, and local government units in adapting environment-friendly processes and technologies incorporating climate change adaptation and mitigation, and disaster risk reduction measures.

Box 1: The Asian Development Bank's Technical Assistance to Support Philippine Issuers and Underwriters

The Asian Development Bank (ADB) is implementing a regional technical assistance (TA) program to develop an ecosystem for sustainable local currency bond market development in Association of Southeast Asian Nations plus the People's Republic of China, Japan, and the Republic of Korea (ASEAN+3). Under the guidance of ASEAN+3 finance ministers and central bank governors, this TA was developed and implemented in accordance with the ASEAN+3 Asian Bond Markets Initiative's Medium-Term Road Map for 2019–2022.

The TA project's objective is to improve a sustainable finance ecosystem in the ASEAN+3 region, including the Philippines. One of the main activities is to increase awareness of sustainable bonds among key capital market participants. In 2021, ADB organized a series of webinars in collaboration with the Capital Market Development Council and with the support of relevant regulatory bodies and industry associations to discuss sustainable bond issuance processes for potential issuers; in-depth deal pitching with underwriters and arrangers; and the development of environmental, social, and governance portfolios for underwriters.

Another key activity is to provide hands-on support to prospective issuers and underwriters to facilitate the issuance of sustainable bonds in the Philippines—from identifying eligible projects, assets, and expenditures to preparing green, social, and sustainability bond frameworks and conducting discussions with external reviewers.

ADB would be happy to provide free consultation and provide technical hands-on support to Philippine companies wishing to issue green, social, or sustainable bonds in the Philippines. For interested entities, please contact Kosintr Puongsophol, financial sector specialist, ADB at kpuongsophol@adb.org.

Source: ADB.

Box 2: The Asian Development Bank's Journey into Green Bonds in the Philippines

One of the key value additions of Asian Development Bank (ADB) in relation to labeled debt instruments is sending a signal to the market that the bonds and loans supported by ADB can be trusted. With our projects, we have ensured from the start that the labeled instruments we have invested in have a high level of integrity by supporting an independent review by a reputable verifier and encouraging certification by the Climate Bonds Initiative.

Our journey in the Philippines started in 2015 when ADB guaranteed a project bond for Tiwi–MakBan, Aboitiz Power Corporation's geothermal power plant complex in the Philippines. Tiwi–MakBan was a groundbreaking transaction. It was the first credit-enhanced project bond in the region since the 1990s and the first climate bond certified in emerging markets for a single project. ADB covered 75% of the scheduled principal and interest payments and shared its exposure with Credit Guarantee and Investment Facility under a risk-sharing agreement. The project received several awards such as the Bond Deal of the Year by Project Finance International.

In 2019, ADB made a USD20 million anchor investment in the maiden climate bond issuance of AC Energy, a subsidiary of Ayala Corporation in the Philippines. This landmark public listing was the first listed Climate Bond Initiative certified US dollar climate bond in Southeast Asia. ADB invested in the 10-year tranche, contributing to a total issuance volume of USD410 million. The proceeds of the bonds financed renewable energy projects in the Southeast Asia region, including Indonesia, the Philippines, and Viet Nam. This climate bond supports AC Energy's plans to establish and expand a regional presence in the development of clean energy projects in accordance with environmental best practice. The project also received several awards such as the Green Deal of the Year by The Asset.

This investment is in line with ADB's Strategy 2030, which mandates that at least 75% of the number of ADB's committed operations support climate change mitigation and adaptation by 2030, with climate finance from its own resources reaching USD100 billion from 2019 to 2030.

Source: ADB.

FINAL WORD FROM SURVEY RESPONDENTS

Survey respondents were asked to give some final words on green bond market development in the Philippines. The following are a few highlights and direct quotes from respondents:

▶ "While Europe and the United States are more mature markets in terms of their ESG journeys, ASEAN is fast catching up. It is important to ensure that the latter's journey stays on track given the comparably lower financial resources that ASEAN countries have."

▶ "The green bond market effectively raised awareness on the beneficial impact of pursuing sustainability across the supply value chain."

▶ "Development of the green bond market will boost the Philippine economy and be a great help to the country."

▶ "Support green and sustainable financing to protect the environment and Mother Earth."

▶ "Philippine investors may need more learning at this stage."

▶ "Looking forward to seeing the green bond market grow in the Philippines and increase awareness among investors with support from public and private institutions and regulators."

▶ "This is a good investment and looking forward for a more improved market for green bonds."

▶ "[We] still have to study, learn, and understand a lot."

▶ "Green bonds and sustainable finance are interesting. It is the future."

▶ "The responsibility of the green bond market development in the region is a collective effort between the public and private sectors."

▶ "Potential is high and there is much room to provide support in terms of technical expertise and promoting continuous awareness to all the stakeholders and at the different levels in the organization of these stakeholders."

▶ "There is still limited issuance in the region."

▶ "Looking forward to [the green bond market's] further development."

▶ "[We] need clear guidance and support from regulator."

▶ "The market is expected to grow further with the implementation of the different governments of various laws and policies to support sustainable finance. Also, tax incentives should be automatic for green bonds."

▶ "We are open to green bond market development in the Philippines."

▶ "We appreciate and support the ADB and World Bank's initiatives. [We] believe there is space to grow and develop the market in the region."

NEXT STEPS

This survey revealed that the majority of respondents are committed to becoming more environmentally friendly, both from an investor and underwriter perspective. Additional efforts, however, are required, particularly in terms of capacity building for relevant stakeholders, expansion of the eligible project pipeline and issuer base, and greater incentives including technical assistance from development partners. Currently, the Philippines's green bond market is dominated by three sectors: renewable energy, sustainable agriculture, and water management. It is critical to further diversify these sectors to provide issuers with more funding opportunities and investors with more investment opportunities.

Noting that a substantial number of investors still lack exposure to green assets, it is crucial for development partners to play a larger role in supporting the expansion of green bond issuances and in equipping investors with the ability to make green investments.

As Secretariat of the Asian Bond Markets Initiative, ADB will continue to work closely with local regulatory bodies to establish and strengthen the ecosystem necessary for Philippines's sustainable finance market development, including capacity building, the publication of guidance notes and handbooks, and technical assistance to issuers on their sustainable finance journey.

www.ingramcontent.com/pod-product-compliance
Lightning Source LLC
Chambersburg PA
CBHW050057220326
41599CB00045B/7449